The Amazing Axolotl

Written by Michèle Dufresne

PIONEER VALLEY EDUCATIONAL PRESS, INC.

The **water** is still.

It looks blank.

But look down, down, down

in the mud.

A pink **axolotl** swims

down there in the mud!

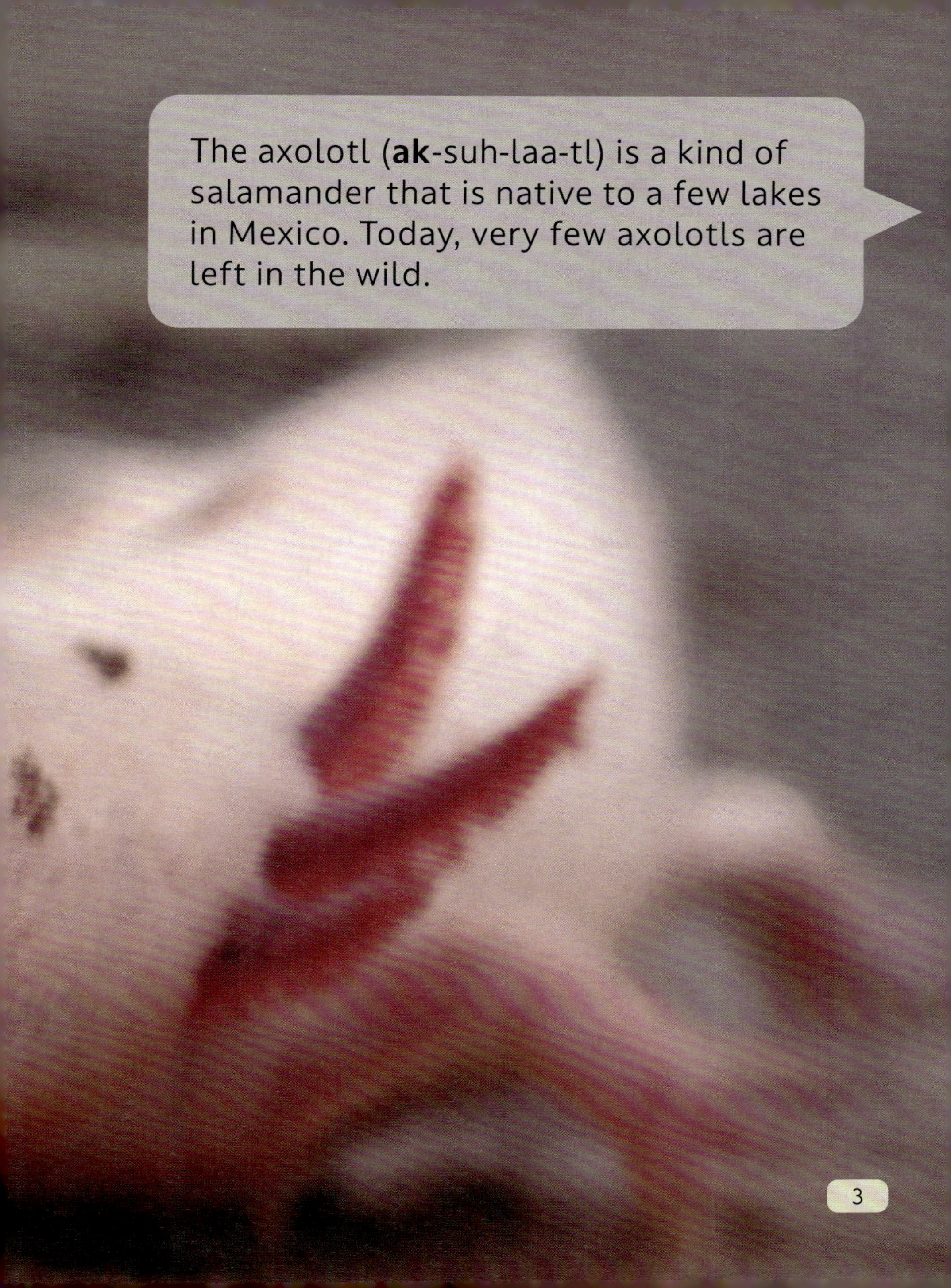

The axolotl (**ak**-suh-laa-tl) is a kind of salamander that is native to a few lakes in Mexico. Today, very few axolotls are left in the wild.

An axolotl has gills.

It has legs.

It will stay in the water.

It does not go on land.

Most salamanders change from tadpoles to adults. This is called metamorphosis. They will go from living in water to living on land. But not the axolotl! It stays in the tadpole state.

Do not fuss if your axolotl gets a cut. It can **grow** new skin! It can also grow new gills!

Axolotls do not blink or wink.

They have no lids on their **eyes**.

Axolotls do not drink water like you and me.

Water goes into their skin and helps them stay well.

Axolotls don't grow eyelids like other amphibians, and their lungs don't fully develop. Instead they keep their gills and use them to breathe.

Do you think that an axolotl
is a good pet?

Yes, it can be a good pet.

Axolotls do not stink.

But their tanks *can* stink.

Axolotls are calm and sweet-natured.
They are also easy to care for. They like to
interact with their owners when it is time
to eat, and they like to explore their tank.

glossary

water

axolotl

grow

eyes